FAITH

The Currency of The Kingdom

Russell Gross

urbanpress

Faith: The Currency of the Kingdom
by Russell Gross
Copyright © 2017 Russell Gross

ISBN 978-1-63360-062-1
For Worldwide Distribution
Printed in the U.S.A.

Urban Press
P.O. Box 8881
Pittsburgh, PA 15221-0881
412.646.2780
www.urbanpress.us

DEDICATION AND ACKNOWLEDGEMENTS

This book is dedicated to my parents, Russell Sr. and Barbara Gross. My mother recently passed into eternity at the ripe old age of 94, but I am blessed to still have my father here who is also 94 and still able to drive. While they both have dealt with physical ailments in their later years, my mother passed without experiencing any pain or suffering, and my father was recently declared by his primary care physician to be in "great shape" for which I am truly thankful. Although my parents were not saved when I was growing up, they instilled in me many of the values that have helped me to become who I am today. They were not regular church goers but always made sure I attended with my grandmother, and at age 93 my father accepted Christ on the last night of a week-long series of services at my church led by Evangelist Ted Shuttlesworth. It's never too late to come to Jesus!

My parents were not wealthy as the world would define wealth, but worked hard as a policeman and nurse to provide a home based on love, honesty, and determination. They taught me these and many other values such as caring, honor, respect, and self-esteem, just to name a few. By their actions, they also showed me what a marriage between a man and woman is supposed to be like, having been happily married for 69 years.

Ephesians 6:1-3 says "Children, obey your parents in the Lord, for this is right. 'Honor your father and mother,' which is the first commandment with promise: 'that it may be well with you and you may live long on the earth." I have tried to live by these Words for most of my life, especially since reaching adulthood. God is my Creator and heavenly Father, but my earthly father and mother are the vessels He chose to bring me into this world and raise me up as to how I should go.

So Mom and Dad, thank you for all you have done for me over the years. I love you both very much, and will always carry you with me in my heart.

I also want to acknowledge the teachings of the many men and women of God who guided me in learning about and exercising faith in the Word of God as I have grown in the Lord. They are too numerous to mention them all here. Some were my pastors, and others were men and women of God whose books I read and whose teachings I followed. All fed me with the Word of God and helped me gain a biblical understanding of what faith is and how it works.

Most of all I want to thank my heavenly Father God for opening up His Word and filling me with revelation knowledge about faith and its role in His Kingdom.

INTRODUCTION

Many people think faith is simply believing, but it's much more than that (and many people don't fully understand what it means to believe, either). James 1:22-25 says we need to do and not just hear the Word. James 2:14-26 says without works (or doing something), our faith is dead. Therefore, if you really want the Word of God to make a difference in your life, you need to exercise your faith by believing the Word in your heart, confessing it out of your mouth, and acting or making movement on what you believe and confess. Simply put, you have to act on what you believe.

Faith is the key, title deed, and access that unlocks and opens the door to all of the promises in God's Word so they can be a reality in our lives. It's what moves God and allows Him to work a miracle in our situations, which in the natural and in our own strength and know-how could never come to pass. It's by faith that we are saved or born again; it's by faith that we are baptized with the Holy Spirit; it's by faith that God moves in our lives; and it's by faith that we experience all God intends for us to be, do, and have in our lives.

In this book, I want to share what I have learned and put into action in my own life in order to help the reader gain a greater understanding of what faith is, how it works, and how to activate it, so you can have access to the benefits God has promised in His Word. My intent is that this book will help you understand the components of faith and why faith is so important, and then help you catch the revelation that faith is a lifestyle and not just something you turn to and apply in times of trouble. This book will also provide insight into those things that hinder the effectiveness of your faith, and what you can do to overcome those hindrances.

But why me? What is it that makes me think I am qualified to speak on the topic of faith, let alone write a book about it? Is it because I've been following the Lord for almost 37 years? Many others have also been following the Lord for that long or longer. Is it because I have been a faithful servant in the Kingdom of God all of these years? Many others have faithfully served in the Kingdom for as long or longer. Is it because I have been promoted in the Kingdom to serve in a variety of administrative and ministry leadership positions in my local church? So have many others. Is it because I have been ordained in the office of elder in the Kingdom? Countless others have also been ordained as an elder and much higher spiritual leadership positions in the body of Christ. Is it because I have studied and caught the revelation of what biblical faith is and tried to live my life as a man of faith in the Kingdom for almost 37 years? Here again, many other brothers and sisters in the Body have done so as well.

First and foremost, the Lord has called me to write this book. Second, I believe it is all of the things I mentioned above collectively that summarize my spiritual journey with the Lord and have required me to walk by faith, making most of the mistakes one could make along the way. All that qualifies me to write this book.

Other men and women of God with much higher callings than I have written books on faith, but I believe God has called me to deliver the faith message from the perspective of a rank-and-file saint. While I have been in leadership positions and am ordained, I am not a pastor, bishop, media evangelist, well-known, faith-based author, or anything along those lines. I am simply an obedient servant in the body of Christ who is not perfect, has made a lot of mistakes, and submits to the spiritual covering of a pastor whom the Lord has called me to come under. In other Words, I'm just like the majority of saints in the Body.

If I have been able to catch the revelation of biblical faith and apply it in my life, allowing God to move me from where I was when He found me to where I am now (and I am still a work in progress), He can do the same for any other of His children. This is why I believe He has called me to write this book and qualifies me to do so.

Through faith, I have been saved, forgiven, filled with the Holy Spirit, healed, provided for financially, promoted, had broken relationships restored, doors opened, and delivered from dangerous situations. Through my faith, I have come to experience and know that God is my source for everything I will ever need. Nothing speaks more to a person's understanding and knowledge of something than their personal testimony. So I have shared a couple of very detailed testimonies in the "Practical Applications" chapter near the end of this book, demonstrating how I applied the principles shared in earlier chapters in my own life.

While I believe these testimonies will have more meaning after you have read the earlier chapters, please feel free to jump to the "Practical Applications" chapter now if you still have questions as to whether or not I know something about what I'm sharing in this book. This book is a short read, so don't let the enemy rob you of what the Lord has for you because of the messenger. I'm just the channel, but it's God who is speaking in this book!

I pray you will be blessed as you read this book.

Then I pray that you apply the principles of faith you learn in your own life on a daily basis, so you can be used for the work of the Kingdom as the Lord intends and receive blessings He wants you to have.

WHAT FAITH IS

Before we dive into how faith works or how we activate it in our lives to claim the promises of God in His Word, we need to first understand what faith is because what faith is and how faith works are two different things.

So let's start defining what faith is by looking at Hebrews 11:1. The first part of this verse says "Now faith is." So the first thing we see is that faith is always present tense, right now, not past or future, but present. Whenever you exercise your faith to claim anything God promises in His Word, you have to believe you receive it now when you ask Him for it in prayer by faith. It may not (and usually doesn't) manifest now in the physical. If you believe you receive it now when you pray for it by faith, however, then you receive it now in the spirit realm. As you continue to exercise your faith through your confessions and actions despite what your circumstances may say, what you exercised your faith for in time will manifest in your life. Then you will know you have it, and no longer have to believe you have it. Faith is always present tense now!

The second part of Hebrews 11:1 says faith is "the substance of things hoped for." Now when something has substance, it's tangible, and can be touched and felt. In other Words, it has materiality and is real. I like one definition of hope, which says it is "the expectation of future good." So as it relates to the things of God, faith is not only always present tense but is also the reality of the future good you're expecting from God based on His Word. Another way to say this is that faith takes the place of what you are believing God for based on His Word, until that thing manifests in your life. First, faith is always present tense. Second, faith is the substance of things hoped for, or the reality of the future good you are expecting from God (based on His Word)!

The last part of Hebrews 11:1 states that faith is the evidence of things not seen. Another Word for evidence is proof, and when there is proof about something, you have confidence in or about that thing. In this part of Hebrews 11:1 what faith is the proof of and gives you confidence about are the things not seen for which you are believing God, the future good you are expecting based upon all of the promises in His Word. Therefore, the third point is that faith is the proof that what you are believing God for (the future good you are expecting) already exists, and instills confidence that you already have it.

When we put these three parts of Hebrews 11:1 together, we could translate Hebrews 11:1 to read, "Whenever I stand on the Word of God, my faith is the reality of the future good I am expecting, the proof that this future good already exists, and the confidence that it will manifest or come to pass in my life." For me, this is another and simpler way of thinking about what faith is, and I pray it helps you better understand it. You can also think of or define faith as trusting God to do what He said in His Word He would do.

Any of these definitions of faith work, but I like the Hebrews 11:1 definition since it better encompasses the three key aspects of activating your faith: 1) believing the

Word God put in your heart without any doubt; 2) confessing that belief out of your mouth and over your life or situation; and 3) acting or making movement on what you believe in your heart and have confessed out of your mouth.

HOPE

Let's talk a little bit more about hope, which is the fuel for your faith. We learned in the previous section after examining the first part of Hebrews 11:1, which says "faith is the substance of things hoped for," that hope is the expectation of future good based on God's Word. So part of faith is the substance or reality of the future good you expect from God based on His Word.

If that's the case, without hope for any future good, there is nothing on which to exercise or focus your faith. No hope, no faith. Therefore, hope is the basis for exercising your faith, or the fuel for your faith engine. Therefore, without hope (in something), there can be no faith.

Now one thing that a lot of people do is mistake hope for faith, believing that hope is the same thing as faith. As a result, these people go around making confessions like "I hope God will heal me," "I hope God brings me together with the mate He's already selected for me," "I hope God cancels my debts," and many other "I hope" statements or confessions. What this says to me is that people really don't know the Word of God or haven't gotten it in their spirit to the point that they truly believe it. If they had done so, they would not be hoping for God to do something He promised in His Word to which every believer is entitled. If they had done so, they would claim that promise (the expectation of future good, or the thing they have hope for) by the exercising of their faith, which we'll look at in a later section.

How do you get hope? If hope is the expectation of future good based upon what God has promised in His Word, then we get hope by having a devotional life and studying the Word of God on a regular basis, preferably daily. By doing so, you will discover and learn all of the wonderful blessings God has promised you in His Word. Then, you'll have hope (the expectation of future good) upon which to exercise your faith daily. You will go on to build up your faith, learning to claim and have all God has promised you in His Word. Then your faith will be well-developed and strong so you can withstand the attacks of faith's enemies.

But, if you don't have the Word in you, you won't have any hope, and without any hope, you can't exercise your faith. No Word, no hope; no hope, no faith, and no blessings. Therefore, study the Word so you have hope, and then exercise your faith on that hope and have the blessings God has promised would manifest in your life.

WHY FAITH MATTERS

Hopefully, the first several chapters of this book helped you see why faith really matters. Now let's take a closer look into this issue of the importance of faith.

Faith matters because while money is the currency of the world or the way we get things done here in the earthly realm, faith is the currency of the Kingdom or the way things get done in the Kingdom of God and how we claim the promises of God. If you desire proof, then let's look at these Bible verses.

Romans 1:17, which tells us that the righteous shall live by faith; 2 Corinthians 5:7, which says that we should walk by faith and not by sight (In other Words, we should live our lives believing, confessing, and acting or making movement on the Word of God instead of our circumstances), James 1:5-8, which directs us to ask God in faith if we need wisdom about anything. What's more, you can read Hebrews 11 to see that faith transcends the Old and New Testaments of the Bible, and there are many more passages that bear this out as well. So why does faith matter? It matters because it's the currency of the Kingdom.

You see, God is a God of faith. He responds to

our faith and not our emotions or how we feel. It's by the exercising of our faith that God acts in our lives to turn around situations that in the natural seem hopeless, because nothing is impossible for God. It is through the exercising of our faith that we are able to appropriate or claim the promises of God in His Word, be it for healing, financial breakthrough, salvation of loved ones, restoration of broken relationships, deliverance from addictions, and on and on. Faith is the currency by which God is moved to intervene in our lives, through which we can have all He says we can have, be all He says we can be, and do all He says we can do. Faith is the currency of the Kingdom of God.

If faith is the currency of the Kingdom, why is it that most people, including a good number of Christians, don't exercise their faith on a regular basis? This happens because of a deception of the enemy who created a world system that operates on money, greed, and self. This is why many people work at jobs they don't like and to which God has not called them. The world system says you must work to make money, and the more you work the more money you will make. You are then deemed a success based on how much money you have because money is king and there isn't anything money can't buy! That lie and others like it have caused most people to become slaves to their jobs under the guise of a career, with money being the end goal and reason why they work.

What do we do with the money we make? Yes, most use it to support their families as they should, but after that, they often indulge themselves and their families in the riches and luxuries of this world. They might save a little, but not enough. They might give at their local church, if they attend one, but most are not faithful tithers and givers.

I could give more examples, but I think you get

the picture. We have gotten away from trusting God as our source (for everything), and have placed our trust in ourselves, our jobs, and material things in the world. We need to get back to trusting God and Him alone as our source, which takes faith. God will use things in the world as channels to provide what we need and desire, but He is our source and should have our complete trust, confidence, and faith if we are going to enjoy the abundant life He's promised us in His Word. Jesus died, allowing His body to be mutilated, to free us from all sickness and disease and to strengthen us. Jesus shed His blood to free us from sin and the bondage and dominion of Satan. We can only walk in healing, freedom, and deliverance, however, as we put our faith in the Word of God.

That's why faith matters!

HOW
FAITH
WORKS

Armed with an understanding of what faith is and why it matters, let's look at how faith works, and answer the question, how do we practically apply faith in our everyday lives? We saw in James 1 and 2 that faith involves works or action, and in Mark 11:24 and Romans 10:9-10 we see that faith also involves believing and confessing with our mouths. So faith works by believing, confessing, and acting on the Word of God, in that order. Let's now look at how each of these three components actually works to help us apply faith in our lives so we can understand what to do and not to do as we seek to exercise faith in our daily lives.

The first thing we must do to practically apply faith in our everyday lives is to believe. When you believe something, you take something as truth. The something we are talking about here is the Word of God. Consequently, to believe as it relates to exercising our faith on the Word of God is to take the Word of God as truth.

In order to take anything as truth, you first have to learn about it, come to know it, and be intimately knowledgeable about it. You must literally have that thing embedded in your spirit. This requires studying it (the Word of God in this case) over and over according to Romans

10:17, which says faith comes by hearing, and hearing by the Word of God, not just once but continually. This is achieved by meditating on the Word of God continually as Joshua 1:8 directs you to do, until you get the Word in your spirit. When you read the Word of God, read it out loud so you can hear it and it gets down in your heart where you understand and welcome it. Once you have it firmly in your heart, you then believe the Word without any doubt and that becomes the foundation for developing and exercising your faith.

You get the Word in your spirit and come to believe it one truth at a time. If you need healing, study what the Word says about healing until you get it in your spirit and come to truly believe it. If you need a breakthrough in your finances, study what the Word has to say about prosperity and money. Whatever promise of God you need to have happen in your life, find it in the Word, study it, meditate on it, get it in your spirit, and come to receive and believe it in your spirit without any doubt!

Then, and only then, are you ready to start exercising your faith on that belief through your confessions and actions. Once you truly believe something, you will act accordingly, whatever it is, and stand by what you believe in your heart. If someone tells you they believe something but act in a manner that is inconsistent with what they say they believe they really don't believe it. What someone truly believes in their heart is what they will do in their life, especially under pressure. Believing is always followed by a corresponding action based on the belief.

Once you have in your spirit and believe what the Word says about an area of your life in which you need a breakthrough, the next thing you have to do to exercise your faith is confess that Word over your life. This is an action because you are doing something based on what you believe. This part (confessing) is so important, and it may help for you to consider a confession as a separate step in the process of exercising your faith. In Genesis 1, you recall that God "spoke" everything on earth into existence. In Romans 10:9-10, the Apostle Paul tells us that to be saved we must not only believe, but also confess that salvation with our mouths.

Finally, in Mark 11:24, we are told that we have to believe we already have whatever we ask for in prayer in order to have it. Obviously, when you ask for something you say something with your mouth, which is another way of making a confession. First John 5:14-15 also tells us that if we ask anything according to the will of God (according to His Word), we can be assured that He hears and we will have what we ask for.

For example, let's say you need healing in your knees. You've done your study in the Word and truly believe it is God's will for you to be healed according to Isaiah 53:5; I Peter 2:24, and 3 John 2 (just a few of the healing passages in the Bible). At that point, you would confess that belief of your healing according to Mark 11:24, believing you have received what you asked for when you pray for it.

Your confession might go something like this: "Father, I have received and believe Your Word in my heart according to (state the promise you believe), and therefore I believe without any doubt it is your will for me to be healed in every area of my life. Therefore, I claim and believe that I receive your healing in my knees right now, believing every cell, bone, ligament, ACL, MCL, and every part of my knees are being fully restored to the original condition You created them in and functioning perfectly just as You intended. I thank You for this healing in Jesus' name. Amen."

You make your confession out of your mouth based on the Word you believe in your spirit. When you speak God's Word that you truly believe over your life, you are claiming the promises in that Word right then and there. They are now yours, and you need to believe you have received them at the time you asked for them or confessed them, even though they haven't manifested in your life yet.

My pastor always says that what comes out of your mouth will live in your life and he is so right. If God spoke things into creation or being and we are made in God's image, what we say or speak will come into being or come to pass as well. That's why we need to watch what we say, and I mean every Word that comes out of our mouth.

You may remember the late comedienne Redd Foxx, who played the father, Fred Sanford, on the old TV show *Sanford and Son*? What did he always say to get his son Lamont to get him to give in to what he (Fred) wanted? "Oh, I think I'm having the big one" referring to a heart attack, followed by "Elizabeth (his late wife on the show), I'm comin' to join you, honey." He must have said this on at least 75% of the episodes he was in during the show's run from 1972 to 1977. Then what happened to him on October 11, 1991? While rehearsing on the set of what was to be a comeback series for him, Foxx actually did have a heart attack. In fact, many on the set, remembering his *Sanford and Son* days, thought he was joking. But he was not, as he died later that evening after being rushed to the hospital. That was a sad ending to the life of a great talent. But I share this only to make the point that what comes out of your mouth does live in your life. And what comes out of your mouth, especially when you are under pressure, is an expression of what you believe in your heart. Believe the Word of God and confess that, not the current state of your circumstances or what the world says about you or your present situation.

Once you do that, you're ready to exercise the third of component of applying faith to claim the promises of God in His Word. You've found a promise in the Word of God you need in your life, you've come to believe it in your heart and have confessed it over your life, and now you are ready to act or move on what you have believed and confessed.

To act is to do something, and an action is a thing done or accomplished, commonly called a deed. To move is to go from one position or place to another. So to act or move on the Word you've believed and confessed with your mouth can be thought of as doing something or going someplace with that belief and confession. It further involves that you continue to confess and make some physical movement despite what your circumstances may indicate. Second Corinthians 4:18. and 5:7 tell us we should be focused on and live our lives based on the unchanging, everlasting Word of God, and not on our temporary circumstances. Our circumstances are real and factual, and we shouldn't deny their existence, but the Word of God is the truth and can change the facts, and is what truly sets us free.

Let's apply this principle of acting or moving on what you believe and have confessed to the example of exercising your faith for healing in your knees. It could look something like this. First, you confess "Father, I thank You, for I believe that I have received healing in my knees, and they are fully restored and function just the way You created them to." Then you would try to use your knees by standing up, trying to walk, bending your knees, or any kind of movement that you couldn't do before. As you keep making this confession and movement each day, you are exercising and building up your faith. As you do, the Word you are standing on will begin to manifest in your life and in time fully manifest. You just need to walk (literally in this case) by faith as you stand on God's Word, and not by the current reality of your circumstances or how you feel.

Now this doesn't mean you stop following the doctors' orders, stop taking prescribed medication or refuse surgery if necessary, because God uses all of these as channels to deliver your healing. Your faith needs to be in the Word of God, however, and not the doctors, medicine, or surgery. This is how you practically exercise faith in your everyday life to receive all God has promised you by following the three steps of believing, confessing, and acting on the Word of God.

If you doubt and think you would get healed over time regardless of what you do, that faith doesn't have anything to do with it, let me share with you a personal testimony from my own life involving healing in one of my knees. I know this may be a bit long, but it is a good, real-life illustration of faith at work.

Nine years ago just after my wife had gone to be with the Lord, I was on a ladder cleaning leaves out of my garage gutters on a warm November autumn day when the ladder gave way, and I tumbled over my deck and tried to land on my left foot. When I hit the ground, I felt my left knee move in a way it isn't supposed to move. There I was on the ground in great pain with no wife in the house to help me. Fortunately, my next door neighbor at the time was a stay-at-home dad, and was out working in his yard. He came over and helped me into the house. I called my son who came and took me to the hospital where a splint was put on my knee, I was given pain killers, and an appointment was made for me to see an orthopedic surgeon.

The surgeon told me I had done damage to the ACL and MCL ligaments and I don't even remember what else. She predicted I would need surgery, but would have to go through rehab first to strengthen the knee. When I got back home, I dug into the Word, reading a number of healing scriptures. Even though I already knew these scriptures well, I wanted to reinforce my belief that it was God's will for me to be healed before I claimed that healing by exercising my faith. Once I did, I confessed those scriptures over my life and claimed healing in my left knee, thanking God when I was done. I then confessed each day that I believed my knee was healed, and tried to move my knee each day even when I couldn't.

I went through the rehab, took the prescribed medications, and saw the orthopedic surgeon regularly as scheduled. Although she would say my knee was getting stronger, she also continued to say my knee was still in pretty bad shape and I would need surgery. My reply was, "Thank you, Doctor, but I believe my knee is healed." This went on for about three months, as I continued to exercise my faith on the Word of God and not focus on the circumstances.

Over time I was able to do more and more with my knee, progressing from crutches to a cane and finally walking short distances on my own. The doctor kept saying I would still need surgery, and I kept saying I believed my knee was already healed. Finally, at the end of the rehab period when I went for what was to be my last exam before having surgery, the doctor asked me to walk on my own, which I was able to do without even a limp. After taking some x-rays, she said she didn't quite understand how, but my left knee was fine. Everything seemed to be back to normal, and she just wanted to drain some fluid build-up out of my knee and I would be good to go, with no need for surgery.

I thanked her and, when I left her office, I thanked God and confessed that I now know (no longer having to believe) that my knee was healed. To this day, my left knee has been just fine, and in fact is stronger than my right knee.

Whether or not you choose to believe it was my faith in the Word of God or just the natural course of events that led to my healing is your choice. I know a lot of people who have gone through a similar experience with their knees, didn't exercise faith, and ended up having surgery, going through several more weeks and in some cases months of rehabilitation before they got most of their mobility back. As for me, I am going to continue to walk by faith in God's

Word believing what He did for me concerning my knee when He gave me back all my mobility!

Let's summarize again these last several points on How Faith Works: We put faith to work in our everyday lives by believing, confessing, and acting or creating action on the Word of God in every area of our lives.

One more thing before we move on. The action part of using your faith also involves "following the instructions." What do I mean by that? You need to understand that whenever you ask God for something, He will always give you an instruction, something you need to do in order to demonstrate your trust in Him that He will do what He said in His Word He would do. Sometimes the instruction doesn't make much sense or doesn't seem to relate to the thing for which you are believing God, but that's part of exercising our faith.

If God said it, take Him at His Word and do what He tells you to do, how He tells you to do it, and when and where He tells you to do it. For example, most times when you are believing God for a financial breakthrough, He will direct you to bless someone else financially, or to sow a financial seed.

How does he tell you? It might be through His Spirit or a man or woman of God, but most times He's already given you the instructions with the promises right in His Word. As it relates to financial blessings, an example of such an instruction along with the promise of financial blessing can be found in Malachi 3:8-12. Read it, believe it, confess it, and act on it, and God will honor your faith.

A LIFESTYLE OF FAITH

There is one aspect of faith that I need to address before moving on to other faith principles, and that is that faith is a lifestyle, not just something we turn to in times of need. Romans 1:17 and 2 Corinthians 5:7 tell us that God's righteousness is revealed from faith to faith, that the just shall live by faith, and we should walk (or live) by faith and not by sight (by the circumstances around us and how we feel). Also, Hebrews 11:6 tells us that we are the just, and cannot please God without living by faith.

God has given everyone the same amount of faith as He tells us in Romans 12:3 (God has dealt to each one a measure of faith). Each of us will determine, however, what we do with that measure of faith. We can use, develop, and grow it so God can move in our lives, or let it sit dormant so that when we really need God to move in our lives, He can't.

His inaction is not because He doesn't want to, but because our lack of making His gift of faith (Ephesians 2:8) a part of our everyday lifestyle limits His ability to move in our lives. Therefore, it is vital that you exercise your faith as a lifestyle, developing and growing it, so you can have God's best each and every day of your life. Faith is not really faith until it's faith! Stated differently, you don't really know how strong your faith is until it's tested.

James 1:2–3 tells us to count it all as joy when we go through various trials and tribulations, because those test our faith and help develop endurance and patience. You see, whenever you exercise your faith for something, there is usually a time element between when you start to exercise your faith and when what you are believing God for manifests in your life. That waiting period requires patience and endurance while you stand on God's Word, exercising your faith despite your circumstances and wait for the manifestation. This is why James 1:4 says that we should let our faith have its perfect work so our patience (and endurance) can be developed, and we can be perfected.

James was not talking about exercising faith for something you want or a need you have, which do require exercising your faith. James was addressing exercising faith when you are under attack by the enemy, which happens to every believer from time to time.

If you haven't been exercising your faith on a regular basis, you will have little or no faith and little or no patience and endurance to be able to withstand the attack of the enemy. But if you do exercise your faith regularly, your faith, patience, and endurance will all be built up and become strong so that you will be able to withstand the attacks of the enemy. This is why I say faith is not really faith, until you exercise, develop, and grow your faith on a regular basis, so it will be strong when you are truly tested by an attack of the enemy.

Therefore, don't get discouraged when trials, tests, and tribulations come your way. Look at them as an opportunity to measure how developed and strong your faith is, and then make it even stronger. After all, why would the devil try to break your faith down if it wasn't a threat to him. That's one reason why 1 Thessalonians 5:18 tells us to thank God "in" (not for) everything!

You have to remember that faith is not really faith until it's faith!

SAY IT OUT LOUD!

How do you develop your faith? Yes, you do have to exercise it on a regular basis as I've mentioned previously, but that's not all. In fact, there's something you have to do before you can even exercise your faith in order to develop it. Let's discover what that is.

Hebrews 11:1 tells us faith is the substance of things hoped for, with hope here being the expectation of future good based on the Word of God. It appears that one needs to know the Word of God in order to have the hope upon which to exercise your faith.

Romans 10:17 tells us that faith comes by hearing the Word of God. One definition of the Word "come" is to move forward toward something. In Romans 10:17, the something being moved toward is the developing, growing, or building up of your faith in the Word of God so you can know it and have hope upon which to exercise your faith. It is not so you can receive or get faith since we know that God has already given us faith as a gift (more on this in the next section when we will look at Ephesians 2:8 and Romans 12:3).

According to Romans 10:17, if you are to move toward developing your faith on the Word of God, you must first hear the Word of God. You can't hear the Word of God, however, until you pick up your Bible and read the Word of God out loud because faith comes by hearing!

Therefore, it's not enough to just read the Word of God silently if you want to develop your faith. You have to say it out loud or confess it out of your mouth, so you can "hear" it, and have it go into your ears and get in your spirit so you can come to truly know it and have hope upon which to exercise your faith. Do you want to develop and grow your faith? Then read the Word of God and "say it out loud," for faith comes or is developed by hearing the Word of God.

Don't only read the Word of God out loud, but also study it and seek God's wisdom as to what His Word means. Look at the same scriptures in different versions of the Bible. Use a concordance and dictionary to help you understand God's Word. Keep in mind that the objective of reading the Word of God out loud and studying it is not only to develop your faith, but also to understand God's Word so you can receive it and believe it in your heart. When you have done so and the enemy comes to try and dissuade, discourage, or convince you to believe his lies, the Word of God is imprinted in your spirit so you can believe and stand on it by faith no matter what his deceptions are.

WHERE DOES FAITH COME FROM?

You must make a conscious decision to use or exercise your faith, but having faith is not a decision you make since faith comes to you as a gift from God. Romans 12:3 says that to each one God has given a measure of faith. The "each one" in that verse includes you, me, and every other human being to whom God has given a measure of faith. You don't decide you want to have faith and you can't earn faith. It is given to us as a gift.

Furthermore, Ephesians 2:8 tells us that faith is not something we earn, but a gift from God. Now a gift is something freely given out of care, concern, or love for another, at no cost with no expectation of anything in return from the recipient. It is given to the recipient to use for their benefit and the benefit of others. Faith is a gift freely given by God to all mankind to be used to benefit His creation.

A gift given is not really a gift until it is received. In other Words, we need to accept, acknowledge, appreciate, and show gratitude toward God for the free gift of faith by using or exercising it as He intends. That use is to be reconciled back to Him through Jesus or to be "saved" (read all of Ephesians 2), to carry out His purpose for your life in order to extend His Kingdom on the earth, and to claim all that

He promises us in His Word for ourselves and others.

I urge you to accept your free gift of faith from God, and use it to carry out God's will for your life, and to be blessed and be a blessing to others. As you do so, you are pleasing God, since faith pleases God! Hebrews 11:6 says that without faith it is impossible to please God. Why? As this verse goes on to say, it is because those who come to God must believe that He exists, and that He rewards those who diligently seek Him. Therefore, if faith pleases God, when you are not exercising your faith, you're not pleasing God.

You see, God is a God of faith, and faith is a gift from God and we show our appreciation for that gift by exercising or using it. God responds when we use our faith, because faith is the currency of the Kingdom of God. It is what we use to get things done in the Kingdom of God and the means by which we appropriate the promises of God in His Word. If we do not exercise our faith, we do not please God and receive no response from God to our prayers.

Also, note the Words used in Hebrews 11:1: *believe* and *diligently seek*. Those Words speak to putting your faith into action—believing God exists and that His Word is truth, and then diligently seeking God by confessing out of your mouth and acting on what you believe in your heart. If you want to please your Heavenly Father, then use the free gift of faith He's given you, make it part of your lifestyle and daily walk with the Lord, be reconciled to Him, and have the abundant life He wants you to have.

Finally, Hebrews 4:16 tells us to come boldly to the throne of grace to find mercy and grace in the time of need. Hebrews 13:6 tells us to speak boldly, that God is our Helper, and not to fear. Ephesians 6:19-20 tells us we should speak the Gospel boldly. Now the Word *boldly* can be defined as not being afraid, lacking fear, and having great confidence. We see from these three scriptures (and there are many more) that God wants us to walk or live our lives with boldness and confidence, which we can do if we follow His Word by faith, just as 2 Corinthians 5:7 tells us to do (for we walk by faith, not by sight).

Therefore, live the life God wants you to live, a life of faith, boldness, and confidence in Him and His Word, and do, be, and have all God wants you to do, be, and have.

FAITH'S GREATEST ENEMIES - INTRODUCTION

The next several chapters, titled "Faith's Greatest Enemies," address deceptions and lies the enemy uses to attack our minds to try and discourage, frustrate, and separate us from our faith. While there are many enemies of faith, there are ten that most everyone will encounter in their walk with the Lord. These are faith's greatest enemies. We need to know what these enemies are so we can be alert, vigilant, and on guard so they don't catch us by surprise and rob us of all God wants us to have. Let's look at these enemies one by one.

Enemy 1: Unrighteous or Unholy Living

This enemy will block and hinder your faith every time, and is not about the righteousness of Christ that we receive through salvation. It refers rather to the righteousness of striving to live a lifestyle of faith in obedience to God's Word.

Deuteronomy 28:1-2 tells us that if we obey God's commandments His blessings will overtake us, while Deuteronomy 28:15 tells us if we do not obey God's commandments, curses will overtake us. This doesn't mean that God curses us, but our disobedience takes us out from under God's covering, His umbrella of protection as it were. It also doesn't mean we have to be perfect to be blessed, because we can never be perfect as long as we live in sinful flesh. What it does mean is that we should strive to live a holy life, a lifestyle of obedience to God's commandments, and when we do stumble and fall, we should confess our sin to God and receive His forgiveness and cleansing available to us through Christ Jesus as 1 John 1:9 tells us.

Don't take what I just explained as a license to sin at will and then keep running back to God and repenting of your sins, thinking all will be well between you and God. As believers or children of God, it's not our nature any longer to sin. That doesn't mean we can't or won't sin, but we should not be able to sin without it bothering us and the Holy Spirit convicting us of our sin. If it doesn't bother us when we sin and we're not convicted, we really need to question if we are truly saved. You can't live with one foot in the Kingdom and one foot in the world.

As 1 Corinthians 10:21 tells us, you can't eat at the table of and drink from the cup of demons and God. You are either all in (with God) or not at all. God wants all of you, not just 90% of you. Sinning doesn't break our relationship with God, but it breaks our fellowship and communion with Him, one of the reasons He created us. Sin prevents Him from moving in our lives and us from claiming the promises in His Word. In other Words, when we are living in disobedience to God's Word or intentionally living an unrighteous or unholy lifestyle, our faith is hindered and rendered ineffective since no sin can exist in God's presence and consequently He will not respond to our faith.

Why does God make forgiveness and cleansing available to us in 1 John 1:9? He does so because He realizes we still live in sinful flesh even though we have been redeemed by Christ. As such, He made provision for us so that if we do stumble and fall, which we all do from time to time, then we just agree with Him that we did so and agree with Him that we need to be forgiven. We can receive what He's already made available to us through Christ, which are forgiveness and cleansing (which includes clearing our conscience of the guilt of our sin that Jesus took away for us), and then get back in fellowship and communion with God. This should be the exception rather than the rule as to how we live our lives. Therefore, strive to live a righteous and holy lifestyle so your faith remains strong, and lay claim to all of the blessings God wants you to have.

Enemies 2 and 3: Doubt or unbelief, and ignorance of the Word

These two enemies of faith go hand in hand, so we will look at them together. We learn in Mark 11:23-24 and Hebrews 11:6 that the first thing we have to do to effectively exercise our faith is to believe the Word of God in our heart without any doubt, which entails believing that God exists and rewards those who diligently seek Him. You may have some doubt in your mind, because that's where the enemy can and does attack you with deceptions, lies, and false doctrine. For your faith to be effective, however, you have to have the Word of God settled in your heart as the truth, the final authority, and absolute rule of conduct for your life.

This third enemy goes right along with the second enemy, and that is ignorance of the Word (of God). You need to get the Word of God settled in your heart so you have no doubt or unbelief regarding God's Word, which re-quires spending time in the Word, meditating on it, study-ing it with the help of other resources like a concordance, dictionary, different versions of the Bible, other people who may have already caught the revelation you are seeking, and of course God, asking Him to open up the scriptures and guide your understanding as to what they mean and how to apply them in your life. When you do these things, the sureness in your heart about the Word will override the doubt and unbelief that may be in your mind. Then, your faith will be strong, effective and work for you as God intended it to.

As I mentioned earlier, you need to spend time in the Word of God, reading, hearing, meditating, and getting it in your spirit so you can first receive it and then you can believe it in your heart (spirit) without any doubt or unbelief, which is the result of falling prey to the trickery and deception of the enemy.

But if you don't spend time in the Word, reading it (out loud) and studying it, you won't know the Word, and ignorance of the Word of God is one of the greatest enemies of your faith for which there is really no excuse. God has clearly revealed His Word to us in the Bible and we have many formats now in written, online, and other formats. It's everywhere! The problem with many of us is that we are too lazy to take the time to pick up the Word and dig into to it. Since God has already revealed His Word to us, He no longer has any tolerance for our ignorance of it as He once did (Acts 17:30). Therefore, if we don't know the Word of God, we can't exercise faith toward it and God can't move in our lives. Therefore, I encourage you to make study of the Word part of your regular (preferably daily) devotional time.

FAITH'S ENEMIES 4 AND 5

Enemy 4: Unforgiveness

This is an enemy of faith that most everyone has encountered, sometimes without even realizing it. There are actually at least four forms of unforgiveness that can hinder our faith from being effective. Mark 11:25-26 tells us that if we do not forgive those who sin against us, God will not forgive our sins. If we don't forgive, we are in sin and our faith is rendered ineffective since no sin can exist in God's presence and therefore He cannot respond to our faith. This is a two-way street though, because if we have sinned against someone, we need to be open to receive their forgiveness, the second form of forgiveness. If we don't, we are also living in unforgiveness.

There is also the forgiveness of all our sins God makes available to all mankind through Christ Jesus. If we don't receive it, we are in unforgiveness. Finally, if God has forgiven us, who are we not to forgive ourselves. If we don't, we are in unforgiveness, sin, and our faith won't work.

In fact, if any one of these four types of unforgiveness are in operation in our lives, we hinder God's ability to respond to our faith, and that is just what the enemy since he comes to steal, kill, and destroy. Therefore, be on the alert, and don't let unforgiveness creep into your life, so your faith will remain strong, and you can claim all God has promised you in His Word.

Ask God to show you any areas of unforgiveness in your life, and then, according to 1 John 1:9, agree with God that you are in unforgiveness. Receive His forgiveness and cleansing, and then if you need to forgive anyone or ask anyone for forgiveness because of what you may have said or done to them, do so. If the person is no longer alive or not accessible to you, forgive them before God if they sinned against you or confess your sins against them before God so He can forgive you. Your forgiveness of others not only lifts the sin committed against you off of them, but also off you!

When we forgive, it doesn't mean that we will necessarily forget, another deception of the enemy (we should forgive and forget). Most times we don't forget and may very well never forget. What forgiveness is all about is letting go of sin, both against you and committed by you, and not holding the sin of those who sinned against you against them or yourself. Instead, you are to have the highest and best interests of those who sinned against you in your heart, praying for them, asking God to touch their hearts and bless them, and continuing to love them (especially a brother or sister in Christ). This doesn't mean you put yourself right back in the same position you were in when someone sinned against you, because even though you forgive them, that doesn't mean they have or will change their ways. You have to love and pray for some people from afar.

Finally, after you've received God's forgiveness for and cleansing from your unforgiveness, you must repent according to Romans 12:2. Ask God to help you change the way you think regarding forgiveness so you can evolve to a point where forgiveness is part of your nature. This is a process and it takes time. You have to replace what the world has drummed into you over the years about holding grudges and not forgiving with what God says about forgiveness, which you do by getting the Word of God into your mind and heart. Study the Word. Let God guide you through His Holy Spirit and catch the revelation of what it truly means to forgive until it becomes part of your nature to forgive.

Enemy 5: Pride

This is probably the greatest enemy of all of faith, and can manifest in one's life in any number of ways. You can think you're better than others; look down on others; blame everybody but yourself (including God) for your shortcomings and failures; be braggadocious; think you don't need anyone's help, including God's; and believe any success you've achieved in life is all your own doing, just to name a few.

When we are prideful, our faith is nipped in the bud. We won't get God's attention and He will not respond to our faith. In fact, if we are prideful, we're probably not operating by faith at all! James 4:6 and 1 Peter 5:5 tell us that God resists the proud. More important than that, Proverbs 6:17-19 tells us there are seven things God hates and are an abomination to Him, with pride being right at the top of the list. One definition of an abomination is extreme disgust and hatred. So if God resists and has extreme disgust and hatred toward pride, do you think your faith will be effective when you are being proud? Absolutely not!

Therefore, humble yourself and submit to God in order to rise about the enemy's trap of pride. Then your faith will be strong and effective, and the future good you are expecting from God will manifest in your life. Second Chronicles 14:7 tells you to humble yourself before God, pray, seek His face, and turn from your wicked ways. Then, God will forgive you, heal you, and hear your prayers.

Humility doesn't mean humiliating yourself or having low self-esteem. It does mean not to think of yourself as better than anyone else because of what may have been achieved in your life, your position or title, or who you are. Rather, put the needs and interests of others above your own, and have an attitude of wanting the highest and best God has for others above your own self-interests without looking for anything in return. Express the agape love of God He has placed inside of you toward others, letting God's light, goodness, and love touch the lives of others through you.

Enemy 6: Lying

Have you ever told an untruth, thinking you were justified in doing so, maybe to spare someone's feelings, or to protect yourself, or to uphold someone's (or your own) honor or reputation? Perhaps it was (as the world likes to call it) just a little white lie. Or, maybe you lied to boast and make yourself look good, which is double the trouble because you mixed lying with pride. Then there may have been those times when you just flat out lied about something and knew you were lying when you said it.

It really doesn't matter, because a lie is a lie is a lie, and lies feed upon lies! I can't find scripture in the Bible that justifies lying. In fact, lying is right after pride in the list of seven things God hates and are an abomination to Him (cause Him extreme disgust and hatred) in Proverbs 6:16-19. If we lie for any reason, our faith is rendered ineffective since God is not going to respond to our faith when we are doing something He hates that causes Him extreme disgust.

Therefore, stop letting the demon spirit of lying be part of your lifestyle! Repent, and change your thinking so your thinking lines up with the Word of God, and speak the truth or say nothing at all. If you do stumble and lie, which you might since we still live in this sinful flesh, confess that lie as sin before God, and receive His forgiveness and cleansing. Then your faith will continue to be effective!

Enemy 7: Gossip

Verses 18–19 in Proverbs 6 describes feet that are swift in running to evil, a false witness who spreads lies, and one who causes discord among the brethren, all of which are on the list of the seven things God hates and are an abomination to Him. Also mentioned is gossip, which in its simplest form means talking about the personal lives of other people.

Gossiping is a form of devilish evil, and involves spreading rumors of untruth about the subject of the gossip, and is usually carried out behind the back of the one being gossiped about eventually causing a rift between that person and those involved in the gossip. In any event, if God hates gossip and it causes Him extreme disgust, you can rest assured our faith is going to be hindered and ineffective if we are involved in gossiping and are trying to exercise our faith.

Stop gossiping! Confess the sin of gossip before God and receive His forgiveness and cleansing. Repent, and change your thinking about gossiping to line up with Proverbs 6:16-19. And if you can't say something good or edifying about a person to others as well as the person themselves, don't say anything. Walk away when people you are talking with start gossiping about someone else. Even better, don't stand for it. If you can stop the gossip, do so. If you cannot, however, just let those involved in gossiping know that it is not right, you cannot participate in it, and walk away. That way you won't disgust God and what you are exercising your faith toward will come to manifest in your life.

Enemy 8: Fear

Second Timothy 1:7 tells us that God has given us

a spirit of power and love, not a spirit of fear. When we are operating in fear, we are not operating in faith, as fear is the opposite of faith. When you operate in faith, you boldly step out believing, confessing, and acting on God's Word with full confidence and assurance that He will do what He said He would do in His Word, without any concern about Him not doing it for any reason. But when you operate in fear, you have concerns that God may not do for you what He said in His Word He would do, or just not do it for you.

Fear is being apprehensive or leery about or not wanting to experience or be exposed to someone, some-thing, or some situation out of concern over possible phys-ical, emotional, social, financial, or economic harm. Fear is also not being sure you can do what God has told you to do (the instructions) to get your breakthrough. On the other hand, faith is the reality, proof of, and confidence in the future good you are expecting from God based on His Word, without any doubt that if you do your part (follow the instructions), God will do His part, which in fact He has already done. If you are in fear, or apprehensive and leery about God being able to do what He promised in His Word for your life, you can't possibly be in faith, and you cannot expect to effectively be able to exercise your faith.

Why then do we fear when we know about faith? It's just another deception sent our way by the enemy to disable us from our faith and keep us in bondage. Therefore, as James 4:7 tell us to do, submit to God! Then you can resist the devil and he will flee from you. That way, you can walk in the spirit of power and love God has given you, rise above the fear with which the enemy tries to deceive you, and move with strong faith operating in your life. We also operate in fear because we haven't exercised our faith on a consistent regular basis. Therefore, it's weak instead of strong when we need it to be strong.

Most people often misquote James 4:7, and many

times only say the part about resisting the devil so He will flee from you. But if we are not first submitted to God and His delegated authorities (whether we agree with them or not, unless they ask us to do something illegal, immoral, or ungodly), then we can resist the devil all day long, but he's not going anywhere, but will continue to discourage, distract, and frustrate us so he can separate us from our faith and rob us of what is rightfully ours through Christ.

It is vital that you exercise your faith daily according to the Word of God to make it strong and able to withstand the attacks and deceptions of the enemy.

FAITH'S ENEMIES 9 AND 10

Enemy 9: Our Circumstances

Circumstances are comprised of everything going on around us each day, our current state or condition, the current state or condition of others, and the current state or condition of the environment around us. Whether good, bad, or indifferent, our circumstances can distract us and get us away from God's Word, and cause us to do or not do something based on how we feel instead of based on what the Word says. When we allow that to happen, the enemy has us right where he wants us, trying to move by what we think or feel and not by faith in God's Word.

One of my favorites passages of scripture, 2 Corinthians 4:18, tells us not to live our lives based on our circumstances, which are real and should not be denied but, because they are temporary, we should instead live our life based on the Word of God, which is everlasting truth, and can change our circumstances.

Another of my favorite passages of scripture in 2 Corinthians 5:7 tells us that we should live our life by faith in God's Word, and not by sight of the circumstances around us. Then our faith will be strong, effective, and bring us the results we are expecting.

Enemy 10: Not understanding
what faith is and how it works

Earlier in this book, we discussed what faith is and how it operates, being two related but different things. Faith is the reality of the future good you are expecting from God, the proof that it already exists, and the confidence that you will come to know you have it. Faith works when you believe, confess, and act on the Word of God. A misunderstanding of these truths is one of the misinterpretations the enemy uses to confuse us about faith and try to keep us from developing and exercising strong faith in our lives.

Many people define faith to be simply believing the Word of God, or that faith is having hope in the Word of God. Many people I have talked to never thought of what faith is and how faith works as two different things. Still others look at faith as waiting on God to do what He said in His Word He would do, without any action on their part. All of this goes back to enemy #3, ignorance of the Word of God. How can we exercise strong faith in our lives if we don't understand what faith is and how it works? How can we understand what faith is and how it works if we don't have knowledge of the Word of God? How can we have knowledge of the Word of God if we don't take the time to read (out loud) and study it?

My pastor urges us regularly not to be ignorant all our lives! The devil loves ignorance of the Word, because when we don't know what the Word of God says about a particular situation or thing, he has us right where he wants us and can easily deceive us into believing what he wants us to believe, thus rendering our faith useless. Let's not be ignorant all of our lives. Read and study the Word, get it in your spirit, and live by that!

OVERCOMING FAITH'S GREATEST ENEMIES

So how do we rise above or overcome these ten enemies of our faith, as well any other enemy of faith not covered in this book? We can defeat them by getting the Word of God rooted in our hearts and developing a lifestyle of faith.

Joshua 1:8 tells us we should meditate on the Word of God day and night and not let it depart from us, then we will prosper and have good success. First Thessalonians 5:17 tells us to pray without ceasing. In other Words, we need to get the Word of God settled in our hearts without any doubt through study and prayer, have a devotional life, and exercise our faith, all on a daily basis. By doing so, we will be able to rise above the circumstances and stay strong in our faith when our enemies come against

If we happen to stumble and fall and are taken in by the deception of any of faith's enemies, we can confess to God that we have fallen and sinned and receive His forgiveness and cleansing as promised in 1 John 1:9. Then, we need to get back up and continue walking by faith, rather than beating ourselves up, thinking God will never forgive us, or thinking that we can never go before God again—all deceptions of the enemy.

The choice is yours. You can live like the world and get swallowed up when faith's greatest enemies come and have your faith rendered useless, surrendering what God promises in His Word. Or you can choose to develop the measure of faith God gives to each of us by exercising it daily, reading and studying the Word daily, and walking in relationship with God each day.

Then, as Joshua 1:8 tells you, you can be prosperous and have good success, rise above faith's greatest enemies, and have, be, and do all God wants you to have, be, and do!

PRACTICAL APPLICATIONS OF FAITH (TESTIMONIES)

The best way to demonstrate to anyone the power of faith in God's Word is through your own personal testimony. Therefore, I want to share two of my testimonies about how I exercised faith upon God's Word to bring about a miraculous breakthrough in my life based on the promises in God's Word. The first testimony has to do with finances, and the second with healing, two areas most of us at one point or another in our lives for which we find=ourselves trusting God.

When I was getting ready to take early retirement from NYNX, the predecessor company to what is now Verizon, I was still in my forties and was much too young to stop working. Until I found a new job, I didn't want to dip into my life or retirement savings to be able to maintain my current lifestyle. I received a pretty good financial package when I took early retirement, including some additional money for unused vacation time, and I was then able to take some time off before I would need to go back to work. I did not live a lavish lifestyle and did not have an endless supply of cash available to me, so I knew I would have to go back to work within 6 to 9 months.

If you study God's Word, you will come to know that it is His will for us to work and provide for ourselves, our families, and the work of the Kingdom. Scriptures such as Acts 20:34, 1 Timothy 5:8, and Galatians 6:6-10 bear this out. I knew it was God's will for me to keep working to support my family and myself, as well as the work of the Kingdom through my local church and other ministries. I meditated on these scriptures and others like them until I got this in my spirit so that I received it and truly believed it in my heart without any doubt. I then confessed those scriptures over my life, claiming full employment for myself in whatever position and organization God would have me to be in. I also spent time thanking God for my full employment, believing I had already received it when I prayed to God for it.

Then the most difficult part of exercising one's faith took place, and that was moving on what I believed in my heart and confessed with my mouth through my continued confessions and actions until the answer to my prayer was manifest in my life. This is where my faith was tested. This is where I learned how strong or not strong my faith was. Like it says in James 1:2-8, that is where I had to count it all joy when my faith was tested to produce patience and steadfastness. I had to continually seek God's wisdom by faith to know what I was to do without doubting He would answer me. I had to follow the instructions He gave me as I trusted Him.

At first after believing and confessing, I believed I had already received full employment and was thanking God for it. I then did those things I knew to do, things like update my resume, post it online, apply for positions in which I was interested, and prepare for interviews, to name a few. I was already blessed since part of my early retirement package included the use of executive outplacement services.

Initially, I was pursuing positions in telecommunications, the industry in which I had my experience, along with related industries. After several months, I admit that I was getting frustrated by not receiving the kind of job offers I was looking for. Despite those circumstances, I kept confessing that I already had full employment and thanked God for it every day, believing I would be reemployed before I had to dip into my retirement savings, and also thanking God for His wisdom on what I should be doing.

One day as I was thanking God for answering my prayers, His wisdom in response to my prayers appeared. God was clear that I should seek employment in other fields unrelated to the ones I had been seeking out, showing me that my business skills were very transferable. He also put it in my heart that I should pursue full-time employment in the nonprofit arena. When I shared this with my outplacement advisor, I thought he was going to fall off of his chair. This was a complete turnaround for me as I had never worked in the nonprofit sector in my life.

He was supportive, and he knew I was going to go down this road anyway since the Lord had told me to do so. Within the next two months after this change, I was fully employed. In fact, God's timing is always perfect as I received my first paycheck from my new position working at the United Way of Massachusetts Bay in Boston just days before I would have had to dip into my retirement savings. God is good! I thanked God for answering my prayers and giving me full employment.

That's not the end of this faith story. While I really liked the job I had, it was not my first nonprofit choice. I had wanted to stay working in the Providence area, and was particularly interested in a nonprofit integrated health care system with which I had had an informational interview. They had no openings to fit my skill set at the time. After working at the United Way for about eight months, I went before God again and simply said that if it was His will for me to stay in the United Way position, I would do so, but that I wanted His wisdom on the matter. Was there anything better He might have for me in the Providence area? God's response or instruction was "don't cut your ties," which I did not do. I kept in touch with the people at the healthcare system based in Providence, kept looking in the newspaper and searching the healthcare system's website and the websites of other non-profits in the Providence area, and also kept exercising my faith by thanking God for my full employment where He wanted me to be and for His wisdom and guidance.

To make a long story short, within two months I was working at Lifespan, the integrated healthcare system in Rhode Island I had been interested in, in a position that was a perfect fit for me. That position also allowed me to be involved in the Providence community, which was something I had also wanted to do. I thanked God for this position. I knew I was where He wanted me to be and was in a position that was perfect for me. The job provided for me and my family, and enabled me to support the work of the Kingdom for the past 19 years. Ultimately, it helped position me, along with other financial blessings God has provided over the years, to be able to retire from the corporate world this past year so I can now focus more time on serving Him.

The other testimony I want to share has to do with healing. This happened about 37 years ago when I was a baby Christian and hadn't been saved for even a year yet. I was still a pretty good basketball player back then and played on the weekends when I wasn't commuting to AT&T in New York from New Jersey during the week. I was also newly married and a new stepfather (although I really don't like using the preface step, as being a father is about raising a child in the things of God as to how he or she should go in their life, and not only about bringing a child into the world biologically).

I injured my left shoulder somehow during a game one afternoon. It was sore, but I thought nothing of it. By the next morning, however, I was in a lot of pain and couldn't raise my left arm up very high and could not lift anything of any weight with my left hand. My wife took me to the doctor and after a series of x-rays and tests, the doctor told me the problem with my shoulder was chronic and would probably persist, and all he could do was give me medication for the pain (again, a discussion for another time as to why he told me this).

I took the medication that was prescribed, which did help with the pain, but I was not able to lift anything with my left hand and arm, and could not raise my left hand above my head. As stated, I was a relatively new believer, but had received enough of the Word to know it was God's will for me to be healed and walk in divine health. I read scriptures such as Isaiah 53:3-5, 2 Peter 2:24, and 3 John 2, mediating on and confessing them to reinforce in my spirit beyond any doubt that it was God's will for me to be healed. Then believing that in my heart, I claimed healing in my left arm and shoulder by my faith in God's Word, believing I had received it when I asked God for it in prayer, and I thanked Him for my healing.

Each day after, I confessed that I believed I had received divine healing in my left arm and shoulder and was walking in divine health, thanking God for it, and then trying to move my left arm and shoulder in ways I couldn't before (the action and movement on what I believed in my heart and had confessed with my mouth). One day went by, one week went by, one month went by, one year went by, but there was no change in my physical condition. I was still confessing that I was healed by faith and trying to move my arm and shoulder in ways I couldn't before the injury. When I would take a shower, I would have to lift my left arm up with my right hand to be able to wash under my left arm.

Finally, one day after seven years and believing and confessing that I was healed, trying to make movement with my left arm and thanking God for my healing, I was taking my morning shower. I tried to raise my left arm up un-assisted, and I was able to do so with no pain. Praise God! I moved my left arm and shoulder around up, down, out, in every why I could think of, and it was fine. I thanked God for my healing, confessing that I knew I was healed (since it had manifested, I no longer had to confess I believed I was healed, because I knew it).

There are a couple of lessons to be learned from this testimony. First, God is a God of faith and always honors His Word if we exercise our faith on it. Second, your level of faith at any given time will determine in large part how long it will take for your prayer to be answered after you believe you received when you prayed for it. I was a baby Christian, a relatively new believer, and hadn't exercised my faith that much, so my faith wasn't developed enough to bring my answer from the spirit realm down to the earth realm as quickly as I would have liked. This is why it is so important to exercise your faith on a daily basis to develop and build it up so that when you need strong faith for yourself or some-one else, you will have it.

Third, when your faith may not be strong enough to bring about the manifestation of the answer to your prayer you believe you have already received, you need to share what you are going through with a few other like-minded believers whose faith is more developed or at least as de-veloped as yours, Ask them to stand in faith with you to bring about the manifestation of your answered prayer sooner rather than later. Matthew 18:18-20 bears this prac-tice out.

Four, and this is primarily for men, don't think you can always do it on your own. When I went through all this,

I knew my wife was praying for my healing, but I never told her I was nor did I ask her to stand in faith with me for my healing. I was a young man at the time, and somewhat bull-headed. I thought I could do this on my own without anyone's help.

Over the years, I have learned that it's not God's plan for any of His children to do it on their own, all by themselves. His plan is that we work and support each other in our walk with Him. This is even more of a lesson for husbands and wives. If spouses are truly to walk as one flesh as man and wife according to Genesis 2:24 and Ephesians 5:31, then they need to walk and support each other in everything, including, and I believe starting with prayer.

I pray these testimonies are helpful to you in getting a better understanding as to how faith works and how to exercise your faith, not only for financial breakthroughs and healing, but for any of the promises in God's Word.

WHAT NEXT?

In this book, I have tried to share my insights into faith that I have learned over the years. Through these lessons, I have come to know without any doubt that God is a God of faith who will always respond as we cry out to Him when we walk by faith according to the plan of faith contained in His Word. What I have shared is not and was not intended to be all inclusive, but what I have shared works each and every time.

If you've been struggling in any area of your life, which most of us have, and you are wondering if God has heard your prayers, take a look at what you have been believing, saying, and doing. Is it consistent with what God says? Do your beliefs, confessions, and actions line up with each other? Have you been operating by faith or by how you feel? Have you given into your emotions or even fear? Do you exercise your faith daily to build it up so that when you need "strong faith" you have it? Are your prayers being answered? Are you seeing the breakthroughs and miracles in your life that you need and have been believing God for? Have you been able to stand in faith when an enemy of faith has attacked you?

If any of your answers to these questions is no, then

I challenge you to apply the principles of faith shared in this book. They are life-changing and can be the difference between answered and unanswered prayer, manifested and un-manifested prayer in your life. Remember, faith is the currency of the Kingdom of God, the way we get things done in God's Kingdom. Therefore, develop a lifestyle of "walking by faith and not by sight" (2 Corinthians 5:7).

Be blessed!

ABOUT THE AUTHOR
RUSSELL B. GROSS, JR

A native Rhode Islander with an engineering degree, Russ has had successful business careers in both telecommunications and healthcare, and has been active in promoting diversity in the workplace and community. Having given his life to the Lord almost 40 years ago, he has freely given of his time and talent, as well as his treasure, being involved in leading men's and prison ministries and chairing the Board of Directors at his local church in Providence, RI. Russ has also developed and taught biblically based-courses on Faith (the basis for this book) and, along with his late wife Beverly, Financial Stewardship (the basis for his first book *Kingdom Prosperity*).

Since retiring from the corporate world, Russell Gross has facilitated strategic planning initiatives and conducted workshops and seminars on financial stewardship for community-based organizations. He resides in Attleboro, Massachusetts, is the father of one adult son, and enjoys playing golf and traveling. He is also the author of *Kingdom Prosperity*.

www.ingramcontent.com/pod-product-compliance
Lightning Source LLC
Chambersburg PA
CBHW060041040426
42331CB00032B/1991